RO
LOW

For the
Union Dead

faber and faber
LONDON · BOSTON

First published in Great Britain in 1965
by Faber and Faber Limited
3 Queen Square London WC1N 3AU
First published in this edition in 1985

Printed in Great Britain by
Whitstable Litho Limited
Whitstable Kent
All rights reserved

Lowell, Robert
For the union dead
I. Title
811'.52   PS3523.089
ISBN 0-571-13544-7

For my friend,
WILLIAM ALFRED

Note

I want to make a few admissions and disclosures. My poems on Hawthorne and Edwards draw heavily on prose sentences by their subjects. "The Scream" owes everything to Elizabeth Bishop's beautiful, calm story, *In the Village*. "The Lesson" picks up a phrase or two from Rafael Alberti. "Returning" was suggested by Giuseppi Ungaretti's "Canzone." "The Public Garden" is a recasting and clarification of an old confusing poem of mine called "David and Bathsheba in the Public Garden." "Beyond the Alps" is the poem I published in *Life Studies,* but with a stanza restored at the suggestion of John Berryman. "Florence" steals a sentence from Mary McCarthy's book on Florence. Poems in this book have appeared in Partisan Review, the London Observer, Encounter, Kenyon Review, Yale Review, The Atlantic, and Poetry. The poem, "Hawthorne," was written for the Centenary Edition of the works of Nathaniel Hawthorne (Ohio State University Press).

R.L.

Contents

Water

It was a Maine lobster town—
each morning boatloads of hands
pushed off for granite
quarries on the islands,

and left dozens of bleak
white frame houses stuck
like oyster shells
on a hill of rock,

and below us, the sea lapped
the raw little match-stick
mazes of a weir,
where the fish for bait were trapped.

Remember? We sat on a slab of rock.
From this distance in time,
it seems the color
of iris, rotting and turning purpler,

but it was only
the usual gray rock
turning the usual green
when drenched by the sea.

The sea drenched the rock
at our feet all day,
and kept tearing away
flake after flake.

One night you dreamed
you were a mermaid clinging to a wharf-pile,
and trying to pull
off the barnacles with your hands.

We wished our two souls
might return like gulls
to the rock. In the end,
the water was too cold for us.

The Old Flame

My old flame, my wife!
Remember our lists of birds?
One morning last summer, I drove
by our house in Maine. It was still
on top of its hill—

Now a red ear of Indian maize
was splashed on the door.
Old Glory with thirteen stripes
hung on a pole. The clapboard
was old-red schoolhouse red.

Inside, a new landlord,
a new wife, a new broom!
Atlantic seaboard antique shop
pewter and plunder
shone in each room.

A new frontier!
No running next door
now to phone the sheriff
for his taxi to Bath
and the State Liquor Store!

No one saw your ghostly
imaginary lover
stare through the window,
and tighten
the scarf at his throat.

Health to the new people,
health to their flag, to their old
restored house on the hill!
·Everything had been swept bare,
furnished, garnished and aired.

Everything's changed for the best—
how quivering and fierce we were,
there snowbound together,
simmering like wasps
in our tent of books!

Poor ghost, old love, speak
with your old voice
of flaming insight
that kept us awake all night.
In one bed and apart,

we heard the plow
groaning up hill—
a red light, then a blue,
as it tossed off the snow
to the side of the road.

Middle Age

Now the midwinter grind
is on me, New York
drills through my nerves,
as I walk
the chewed-up streets.

At forty-five,
what next, what next?
At every corner,
I meet my Father,
my age, still alive.

Father, forgive me
my injuries,
as I forgive
those I
have injured!

You never climbed
Mount Sion, yet left
dinosaur
death-steps on the crust,
where I must walk.

The Scream

(derived from Elizabeth Bishop's story *In the Village*)

A scream, the echo of a scream,
now only a thinning echo . . .
As a child in Nova Scotia,
I used to watch the sky,
Swiss sky, too blue, too dark.

A cow drooled green grass strings,
made cow flop, *smack, smack, smack!*
and tried to brush off its flies
on a lilac bush—all,
forever, at one fell swoop!

In the blacksmith's shop,
the horseshoes sailed through the dark,
like bloody little moons,
red-hot, hissing, protesting,
as they drowned in the pan.

Back and away and back!
Mother kept coming and going—
with me, without me!
Mother's dresses were black
or white, or black-and-white.

One day she changed to purple,
and left her mourning. At the fitting,
the dressmaker crawled on the floor,
eating pins, like Nebuchadnezzar
on his knees eating grass.

Drummers sometimes came
selling gilded red
and green books, unlovely books!
The people in the pictures
wore clothes like the purple dress.

Later, she gave the scream,
not even loud at first . . .
When she went away I thought
"But you can't love everyone,
your heart won't let you!"

A scream! But they are all gone,
those aunts and aunts, a grandfather,
a grandmother, my mother—
even her scream—too frail
for us to hear their voices long.

The Mouth of the Hudson

(For Esther Brooks)

A single man stands like a bird-watcher,
and scuffles the pepper and salt snow
from a discarded, gray
Westinghouse Electric cable drum.
He cannot discover America by counting
the chains of condemned freight-trains
from thirty states. They jolt and jar
and junk in the siding below him.
He has trouble with his balance.
His eyes drop,
and he drifts with the wild ice
ticking seaward down the Hudson,
like the blank sides of a jig-saw puzzle.

The ice ticks seaward like a clock.
A Negro toasts
wheat-seeds over the coke-fumes
of a punctured barrel.
Chemical air
sweeps in from New Jersey,
and smells of coffee.

Across the river,
ledges of suburban factories tan
in the sulphur-yellow sun
of the unforgivable landscape.

Fall 1961

Back and forth, back and forth
goes the tock, tock, tock
of the orange, bland, ambassadorial
face of the moon
on the grandfather clock.

All autumn, the chafe and jar
of nuclear war;
we have talked our extinction to death.
I swim like a minnow
behind my studio window.

Our end drifts nearer,
the moon lifts,
radiant with terror.
The state
is a diver under a glass bell.

A father's no shield
for his child.
We are like a lot of wild
spiders crying together,
but without tears.

Nature holds up a mirror.
One swallow makes a summer.
It's easy to tick
off the minutes,
but the clockhands stick.

Back and forth!
Back and forth, back and forth—
my one point of rest
is the orange and black
oriole's swinging nest!

Florence

(For Mary McCarthy)

I long for the black ink,
cuttlefish, April, Communists
and brothels of Florence—
everything, even the British
fairies who haunted the hills,
even the chills and fever
that came once a month
and forced me to think.
The apple was more human there than here,
but it took a long time for the blinding
golden rind to mellow.

How vulnerable the horseshoe crabs
dredging the bottom like flat-irons
in their antique armor,
with their swordgrass blackbone tails,
made for a child to grab
and throw strangling ashore!

Oh Florence, Florence, patroness
of the lovely tyranicides!
Where the tower of the Old Palace
pierces the sky
like a hypodermic needle,
Perseus, David and Judith,
lords and ladies of the Blood,
Greek demi-gods of the Cross,
rise sword in hand
above the unshaven,
formless decapitation
of the monsters, tubs of guts,
mortifying chunks for the pack.
Pity the monsters!
Pity the monsters!
Perhaps, one always took the wrong side—
Ah, to have known, to have loved
too many Davids and Judiths!
My heart bleeds black blood for the monster.
I have seen the Gorgon.
The erotic terror
of her helpless, big bosomed body
lay like slop.
Wall-eyed, staring the despot to stone,
her severed head swung
like a lantern in the victor's hand.

The Lesson

No longer to lie reading *Tess of the d'Urbervilles,*
while the high, mysterious squirrels
rain small green branches on our sleep!

All that landscape, one likes to think it died
or slept with us, that we ourselves died
or slept then in the age and second of our habitation.

The green leaf cushions the same dry footprint,
or the child's boat luffs in the same dry chop,
and we are where we were. We were!

Perhaps the trees stopped growing in summer amnesia;
their day that gave them veins is rooted down—
and the nights? They are for sleeping now as then.

Ah the light lights the window of my young night,
and you never turn off the light,
while the books lie in the library, and go on reading.

The barberry berry sticks on the small hedge,
cold slits the same crease in the finger,
the same thorn hurts. The leaf repeats the lesson.

Those Before Us

They are all outline, uniformly gray,
unregenerate arrowheads sloughed up by the path here,
or in the corners of the eye, they play
their thankless, fill-in roles. They never were.

Wormwood on the veranda! Plodding needles
still prod the coarse pink yarn into a dress.
The muskrat that took a slice of your thumb still huddles,
a mop of hair and a heart-beat on the porch—

there's the tin wastebasket where it learned to wait
for us playing dead, the slats it mashed in terror,
its spoor of cornflakes, and the packing crate
it furiously slashed to matchwood to escape.

Their chairs were *ex cathedra,* yet if you draw back the blinds,
(as full of windows as a fishnet now)
you will hear them conspiring, slapping hands
across the bent card-table, still leaf-green.

Vacations, stagnant growth. But in the silence,
some one lets out his belt to breathe, some one
roams in negligee. Bless the confidence
of their sitting unguarded there in stocking feet.

Sands drop from the hour-glass waist and swallow tail.
We follow their gunshy shadows down the trail—
those before us! Pardon them for existing.
We have stopped watching them. They have stopped watching.

Eye and Tooth

My whole eye was sunset red,
the old cut cornea throbbed,
I saw things darkly,
as through an unwashed goldfish globe.

I lay all day on my bed.
I chain-smoked through the night,
learning to flinch
at the flash of the matchlight.

Outside, the summer rain,
a simmer of rot and renewal,
fell in pinpricks.
Even new life is fuel.

My eyes throb.
Nothing can dislodge
the house with my first tooth
noosed in a knot to the doorknob.

Nothing can dislodge
the triangular blotch
of rot on the red roof,
a cedar hedge, or the shade of a hedge.

No ease from the eye
of the sharp-shinned hawk in the birdbook there,
with reddish brown buffalo hair
on its shanks, one ascetic talon

clasping the abstract imperial sky.
It says:
an eye for an eye,
a tooth for a tooth.

No ease for the boy at the keyhole,
his telescope,
when the women's white bodies flashed
in the bathroom. Young, my eyes began to fail.

Nothing! No oil
for the eye, nothing to pour
on those waters or flames.
I am tired. Everyone's tired of my turmoil.

Alfred Corning Clark

(1916–1961)

You read the *New York Times*
every day at recess,
but in its dry
obituary, a list
of your wives, nothing is news,
except the ninety-five
thousand dollar engagement ring
you gave the sixth.
Poor rich boy,
you were unseasonably adult
at taking your time,
and died at forty-five.
Poor Al Clark,
behind your enlarged,
hardly recognizable photograph,
I feel the pain.
You were alive. You are dead.
You wore bow-ties and dark
blue coats, and sucked
wintergreen or cinnamon lifesavers
to sweeten your breath.

There must be something—
some one to praise
your triumphant diffidence,
your refusal of exertion,
the intelligence
that pulsed in the sensitive,
pale concavities of your forehead.
You never worked,
and were third in the form.
I owe you something—
I was befogged,
and you were too bored,
quick and cool to laugh.
You are dear to me, Alfred;
our reluctant souls united
in our unconventional
illegal games of chess
on the St. Mark's quadrangle.
You usually won—
motionless
as a lizard in the sun.

Child's Song

My cheap toy lamp
gives little light
all night, all night,
when my muscles cramp.

Sometimes I touch your hand
across my cot,
and our fingers knot,
but there's no hand

to take me home—
no Carribean
island, where even
the shark is at home.

It must be heaven.
There on that island
the white sand shines
like a birchwood fire.

Help, saw me in two,
put me on the shelf!
Sometimes the little muddler
can't stand itself!

Epigram

(For Hannah Arendt)

Think of Leonidas perhaps and the hoplites
glittering with liberation,
as they combed one another's golden Botticellian
hair at Thermopylae—friends and lovers,
the bride and the bridegroom—
and moved into position to die.

Law

Under one law,
or two,
to lie unsleeping,
still sleeping on the battlefield . . .

On Sunday mornings,
I used to foray
bass-plugging out of season on
the posted reservoirs.

Outside the law.
At every bend I saw
only the looping shore
of nature's monotonous backlash.

The same. The same.
Then once, in a flash,
fresh ground, though trodden,
a man-made landscape.

A Norman canal
shot through razored green lawns;
black reflecting water arched
little sky-hung bridges of unhewn stone—

outside the law:
black, gray, green and blue,
water, stone, grass and sky,
and each unique set stone!

The Public Garden

Burnished, burned-out, still burning as the year
you lead me to our stamping ground.
The city and its cruising cars surround
the Public Garden. All's alive—
the children crowding home from school at five,
punting a football in the bricky air,
the sailors and their pick-ups under trees
with Latin labels. And the jaded flock
of swanboats paddles to its dock.
The park is drying.
Dead leaves thicken to a ball
inside the basin of a fountain, where
the heads of four stone lions stare
and suck on empty fawcets. Night
deepens. From the arched bridge, we see
the shedding park-bound mallards, how they keep
circling and diving in the lanternlight,
searching for something hidden in the muck.
And now the moon, earth's friend, that cared so much
for us, and cared so little, comes again—
always a stranger! As we walk,
it lies like chalk
over the waters. Everything's aground.

Remember summer? Bubbles filled
the fountain, and we splashed. We drowned
in Eden, while Jehovah's grass-green lyre
was rustling all about us in the leaves
that gurgled by us, turning upside down . . .
The fountain's failing waters flash around
the garden. Nothing catches fire.

Lady Ralegh's Lament
1618

Sir Walter, oh, oh, my own Sir Walter—
the sour Tower and the Virgin Queen's garden close
are deflowered and gone now . . .
Horrible the connoisseur tyrant's querulous strut;
an acorn dances in a girdle of green oak leaves
up the steps to the scaffold to the block,
square bastard of an oak. Clearly, clearly,
the Atlantic whitens to merge Sir Walter's head,
still dangling in its scarlet, tangled twine,
as if beseeching voyage. Voyage?
Down and down; the compass needle dead on terror.

Going to and fro

It's authentic perhaps
to have been there, if now
you could loll on the ledge for a moment,
sunning like a couple,
and look down at the gaps—
if you could for a moment . . .

One step, two steps, three steps:
the hot-dog and coca cola bar,
the Versailles steps,
the Puritan statue—
if you could get through the Central Park
by counting . . .

But the intestines shiver,
the ferry saloon thugs with your pain
across the river—pain,
suffering without purgation,
the back-track of the screw.
But you had instants,

to give the devil his due—
he and you
once dug it all out of the dark
unconscious bowels of the nerves:
pure gold, the root of evil,
sunshine that gave the day a scheme.

And now? Ah Lucifer!
how often you wanted your fling
with those French girls, Mediterranean
luminaries, Mary, Myrtho, Isis—
as far out as the sphynx!
The love that moves the stars

moved you!
It set you going to and fro
and up and down—
If you could get loose
from the earth by counting
your steps to the noose . . .

Myopia: a Night

Bed, glasses off, and all's
ramshackle, streaky, weird
for the near-sighted, just
a foot away.
          The light's
still on an instant. Here
are the blurred titles, here
the books are blue hills, browns,
greens, fields, or color.
                  This
is the departure strip,
the dream-road. Whoever built it
left numbers, words and arrows.
He had to leave in a hurry.

I see
a dull and alien room,
my cell of learning,

white, brightened by white pipes,
ramrods of steam . . . I hear
the lonely metal breathe
and gurgle like the sick.
And yet my eyes avoid
that room. No need to see.
No need to know I hoped
its blank, foregoing whiteness
would burn away the blur,
as my five senses clenched
their teeth, thought stitched to thought,
as through a needle's eye . . .

I see the morning star . . .

Think of him in the Garden,
that seed of wisdom, Eve's
seducer, stuffed with man's
corruption, stuffed with triumph:
Satan triumphant in
the Garden! In a moment,
all that blinding brightness
changed into a serpent,
lay grovelling on its gut.

What has disturbed this household?
Only a foot away,
the familiar faces blur.
At fifty we're so fragile,
a feather . . .

The things of the eye are done.
On the illuminated black dial,
green ciphers of a new moon—
one, two, three, four, five, six!
I breathe and cannot sleep.
Then morning comes,
saying, "This was a night."

Returning

Homecoming to the sheltered little resort,
where the members of my gang
are bald-headed, in business,
and the dogs still know me by my smell . . .
It's rather a dead town
after my twenty years' mirage.

Long awash,
breaking myself against the surf,
touching bottom, rushed
by the green go-light
of those nervous waters, I found
my exhaustion, the light of the world.

Nothing is deader than this small town main street,
where the venerable elm sickens, and hardens
with tarred cement, where no leaf
is born, or falls, or resists till winter.

But I remember its former fertility,
how everything came out clearly
in the hour of credulity
and young summer, when this street
was already somewhat overshaded,
and here at the altar of surrender,
I met you,
the death of thirst in my brief flesh.

That was the first growth,
the heir of all my minutes,
the victim of every ramification—
more and more it grew green, and gave too much shelter.

And now at my homecoming,
the barked elms stand up like sticks along the street.
I am a foot taller than when I left,
and cannot see the dirt at my feet.

Yet sometimes I catch my vague mind
circling with a glazed eye
for a name without a face, or a face without a name,
and at every step,
I startle them. They start up,
dog-eared, bald as baby birds.

The Drinker

The man is killing time—there's nothing else.
No help now from the fifth of Bourbon
chucked helter-skelter into the river,
even its cork sucked under.

Stubbed before-breakfast cigarettes
burn bull's-eyes on the bedside table;
a plastic tumbler of alka seltzer
champagnes in the bathroom.

No help from his body, the whale's
warm-hearted blubber, foundering down
leagues of ocean, gasping whiteness.
The barbed hooks fester. The lines snap tight.

When he looks for neighbors, their names blur in the window,
his distracted eye sees only glass sky.
His despair has the galvanized color
of the mop and water in the galvanized bucket.

Once she was close to him
as water to the dead metal.

He looks at her engagements inked on her calendar.
A list of indictments.
At the numbers in her thumbed black telephone book.
A quiver full of arrows.

Her absence hisses like steam,
the pipes sing . . .
even corroded metal somehow functions.
He snores in his iron lung,

and hears the voice of Eve,
beseeching freedom from the Garden's
perfect and ponderous bubble. No voice
outsings the serpent's flawed, euphoric hiss.

The cheese wilts in the rat-trap,
the milk turns to junket in the cornflakes bowl,
car keys and razor blades
shine in an ashtray.

Is he killing time? Out on the street,
two cops on horseback clop through the April rain
to check the parking meter violations—
their oilskins yellow as forsythia.

Hawthorne

Follow its lazy main street lounging
from the alms house to Gallows Hill
along a flat, unvaried surface
covered with wooden houses
aged by yellow drain
like the unhealthy hair of an old dog.
You'll walk to no purpose
in Hawthorne's Salem.

I cannot resilver the smudged plate.

I drop to Hawthorne, the customs officer,
measuring coal and mostly trying to keep warm—
to the stunted black schooner,
the dismal South-end dock,
the wharf-piles with their fungus of ice.
On State Street
a steeple with a glowing dial-clock
measures the weary hours,
the merciless march of professional feet.

Even this shy distrustful ego
sometimes walked on top of the blazing roof,
and felt those flashes
that char the discharged cells of the brain.

Look at the faces—
Longfellow, Lowell, Holmes and Whittier!
Study the grizzled silver of their beards.
Hawthorne's picture,
however, has a blond mustache
and golden General Custer scalp.
He looks like a Civil War officer.
He shines in the firelight. His hard
survivor's smile is touched with fire.

Leave him alone for a moment or two,
and you'll see him with his head
bent down, brooding, brooding,
eyes fixed on some chip,
some stone, some common plant,
the commonest thing,
as if it were the clue.
The disturbed eyes rise,
furtive, foiled, dissatisfied
from meditation on the true
and insignificant.

Jonathan Edwards in Western Massachusetts

Edwards' great millstone and rock
of hope has crumbled, but the square
white houses of his flock
stand in the open air,

out in the cold,
like sheep outside the fold.
Hope lives in doubt.
Faith is trying to do without

faith. In western Massachusetts,
I could almost feel the frontier
crack and disappear.
Edwards thought the world would end there.

We know how the world will end,
but where is paradise, each day farther
from the Pilgrim's blues for England
and the Promised Land.

*Was it some country house
that seemed as if it were
Whitehall, if the Lord were there?
so nobly did he live.*

Gardens designed
that the breath of flowers in the wind,
or crushed underfoot,
came and went like warbling music?

Bacon's great oak grove
he refused to sell,
when he fell,
saying, "Why should I sell my feathers?"

Ah paradise! Edwards,
I would be afraid
to meet you there as a shade.
We move in different circles.

As a boy, you built a booth
in a swamp for prayer;
lying on your back,
you saw the spiders fly,

basking at their ease,
swimming from tree to tree—
so high, they seemed tacked to the sky.
You knew they would die.

Poor country Berkeley at Yale,
you saw the world was soul,
the soul of God! The soul
of Sarah Pierrepont!

So filled with delight in the Great Being,
she hardly cared for anything—
walking the fields, sweetly singing,
conversing with some one invisible.

Then God's love shone in sun, moon and stars,
on earth, in the waters,
in the air, in the loose winds,
which used to greatly fix your mind.

Often she saw you come home from a ride
or a walk, your coat dotted with thoughts
you had pinned there
on slips of paper.

You gave
her Pompey, a Negro slave,
and eleven children.
Yet people were spiders

in your moment of glory,
at the Great Awakening—"Alas, how many
in this very meeting house are more than likely
to remember my discourse in hell!"

The meeting house remembered!
You stood on stilts in the air,
but you fell from your parish.
"All rising is by a winding stair."

On my pilgrimage to Northampton,
I found no relic,
except the round slice of an oak
you are said to have planted.

It was flesh-colored, new,
and a common piece of kindling,
only fit for burning.
You too must have been green once.

White wig and black coat,
all cut from one cloth,
and designed
like your mind!

I love you faded,
old, exiled and afraid
to leave your last flock, a dozen
Houssatonic Indian children;

afraid to leave
all your writing, writing, writing,
denying the Freedom of the Will.
You were afraid to be president

of Princeton, and wrote:
"My deffects are well known;
I have a constitution
peculiarly unhappy:

flaccid solids,
vapid, sizzy, scarse fluids,
causing a childish weakness,
a low tide of spirits.

I am contemptible,
stiff and dull.

Why should I leave behind
my delight and entertainment,
those studies
that have swallowed up my mind?"

Tenth Muse

Tenth Muse, Oh my heart-felt Sloth,
how often now you come to my bed,
thin as a canvas in your white and red
check dresses like a table cloth,
my Dearest, settling like my shroud!

Yes, yes, I ought to remember Moses
jogging down on his mule from the Mount
with the old law, the old mistake,
safe in his saddlebags, and chiselled
on the stones we cannot bear or break.

Here waiting, here waiting for an answer
from this malignant surf of unopened letters,
always reaching land too late,
as fact and abstraction accumulate,
and the signature fades from the paper—

I like to imagine it must have been simpler
in the days of Lot,
or when Greek and Roman picturebook
gods sat combing their golden beards,
each on his private hill or mountain.

But I suppose even God was born
too late to trust the old religion—
all those settings out
that never left the ground,
beginning in wisdom, dying in doubt.

The Neo-Classical Urn

I rub my head and find a turtle shell
stuck on a pole,
each hair electrical
with charges, and the juice alive
with ferment. Bubbles drive
the motor, always purposeful . . .
Poor head!
How its skinny shell once hummed,
as I sprinted down the colonnade
of bleaching pines, cylindrical
clipped trunks without a twig between them. Rest!
I could not rest. At full run on the curve,
I left the caste stone statue of a nymph,
her soaring armpits and her one bare breast,
gray from the rain and graying in the shade,
as on, on, in sun, the pathway now a dyke,
I swerved between two water bogs,
two seins of moss, and stooped to snatch
the painted turtles on dead logs.

In that season of joy,
my turtle catch
was thirty-three,
dropped splashing in our garden urn,
like money in the bank,
the plop and splash
of turtle on turtle,
fed raw gobs of hash . . .

Oh neo-classical white urn, Oh nymph,
Oh lute! The boy was pitiless who strummed
their elegy,
for as the month wore on,
the turtles rose,
and popped up dead on the stale scummed
surface—limp wrinkled heads and legs withdrawn
in pain. What pain? A turtle's nothing. No
grace, no cerebration, less free will
than the mosquito I must kill—
nothings! Turtles! I rub my skull,
that turtle shell,
and breathe their dying smell,
still watch their crippled last survivors pass,
and hobble humpbacked through the grizzled grass.

Caligula

My namesake, Little Boots, Caligula,
you disappoint me. Tell me what I saw
to make me like you when we met at school?
I took your name—poor odd-ball, poor spoiled fool,
my prince, young innocent and bowdlerized!
Your true face sneers at me, mean, thin, agonized,
the rusty Roman medal where I see
my lowest depths of possibility.

What can be salvaged from your life? A pain
that gently darkens over heart and brain,
a fairy's touch, a cobweb's weight of pain,
now makes me tremble at your right to live.
I live your last night. Sleepless fugitive,
your purple bedclothes and imperial eagle
grow so familiar they are home. Your regal
hand accepts my hand. You bend my wrist,
and tear the tendons with your strangler's twist . . .
You stare down hallways, mile on stoney mile,
where statues of the gods return your smile.

Why did you smash their heads and give them yours?
You hear your household panting on all fours,
and itemize your features—sleep's old aide!
Item: your body hairy, badly made,
head hairless, smoother than your marble head;
Item: eyes hollow, hollow temples, red
cheeks rough with rouge, legs spindly, hands that leave
a clammy snail's trail on your soggy sleeve . . .
a hand no hand will hold . . . nose thin, thin neck—
you wish the Romans had a single neck!

Small thing, where are you? Child, you sucked your thumb,
and could not sleep unless you hugged the numb
and wooly-witted toys of your small zoo.
There was some reason then to fondle you
before you found the death-mask for your play.
Lie very still, sleep with clasped hands, and pray
for nothing, Child! Think, even at the end,
good dreams were faithful. You betray no friend
now that no animal will share your bed.
Don't think! . . . And yet the God Adonis bled
and lay beside you, forcing you to strip.
You felt his gored thigh spurting on your hip.
Your mind burned, you were God, a thousand plans
ran zig-zag, zig-zag. You began to dance
for joy, and called your menials to arrange
deaths for the gods. You worshipped your great change,
took a cold bath, and rolled your genitals
until they shrank to marbles . . .

fattened for your arena suffered less
than you in dying—yours the lawlessness
of something simple that has lost its law,
my namesake, and the last Caligula.

The Severed Head

Shoes off and necktie, hunting the desired
butterfly here and there without success,
I let nostalgia drown me. I was tired
of pencilling the darker passages,
and let my ponderous Bible strike the floor.
My house was changing to a lost address,
the nameplate fell like a horse-shoe from the door,
where someone, hitting nails into a board,
had set his scaffolding. I heard him pour
mortar to seal the outlets, as I snored,
watching the knobbed, brown, wooden chandelier,
slicing the silence on a single cord.
In the low sun, about to disappear,
each branch was like a stocking-stretcher, cut
into a gryphon clawing upward. Here
and there, dull guilding pocked a talon. What
I imagined was a spider crab, my small
chance of surviving in this room. Its shut
windows had sunken into solid wall.

I nursed my last clear breath of oxygen,
there, waiting for the chandelier to fall,
tentacles clawing for my jugular. Then
a man came toward me with a manuscript,
scratching in last revisions with a pen
that left no markings on the page, yet dripped
a red ink dribble on us, as he pressed
the little strip of plastic tubing clipped
to feed it from his heart. His hand caressed
my hand a moment, settled like a toad,
lay clammy, comfortable, helpless, and at rest,
although his veins seemed pulsing to explode.
His suit was brushed and pressed too savagely;
one sleeve was shorter than his shirt, and showed
a glassy cuff-link with a butterfly
inside. Nothing about him seemed to match,
and yet I saw the bouillon of his eye
was the same color as his frayed mustache,
too brown, too bushy, lifted from an age
when people wore mustaches. On each lash,
a tear had snowballed. Then he shook his page,
tore it to pieces, and began to twist
and trample on the mangle in his rage.

"Sometimes I ask myself, if I exist,"
he grumbled, and I saw a sheet of glass
had fallen inches from us, and just missed
halving our bodies, and behind it grass-
green water flushed the glass, and fast fish stirred
and panted, ocean butterflies. A mass
of shadows followed them like moths, and blurred
tentacles, thirsting for a drop of life,
panted with calm inertia. Then I heard
my friend unclasp a rusty pocket-knife.
He cut out squares of paper, made a stack,
and formed the figure of his former wife:
Square head, square feet, square hands, square breasts, square
    back.

He left me. While the light began to fail,
I read my Bible till the page turned black.
The pitying, brute, doughlike face of Jael
watched me with sad inertia, as I read—
Jael hammering and hammering her nail
through Sisera's idolatrous, nailed head.

Her folded dress lay underneath my head.

Beyond the Alps

"Au delà les Alpes est l'Italie," Napoleon 1797

(ON THE TRAIN FROM ROME TO PARIS, 1950, THE YEAR PIUS XII
DEFINED THE DOGMA OF MARY'S BODILY ASSUMPTION)

Reading how even the Swiss had thrown the sponge
in once again, and Everest was still
unscaled, I watched our Paris pullman lunge,
mooning across the fallow Alpine snow—
O bella Roma! I saw our stewards go
foreward on tiptoe banging on their gongs.
Man changed to landscape. Much against my will,
I left the City of God where it belongs.
There the skirt-mad Mussolini unfurled
the eagle of Caesar. He was one of us
only, pure prose. I envy the conspicuous
waste of our grandparents on their grand tours—
long-haired Victorian sages accepted the universe,
while breezing on their trust funds through the world.

55

When the Vatican màde Mary's Assumption dogma,
the crowds at San Pietro screamed *Papa!*
The Holy Father dropped his shaving glass,
and listened. His electric razor purred,
his pet canary chirped on his right hand.
The lights of science couldn't hold a candle
to Mary risen, gorgeous as a jungle bird!
But who believed this? Who could understand?
Pilgrims still kissed Saint Peter's brazen sandal.
The Duce's lynched, bare, booted skull still spoke.
God herded his people to the *coup de grace*—
the costumed Switzers sloped their pikes to push.
Oh Pius, through the monstrous human crush . . .

I thought of Ovid. For in Caesar's eyes
that tomcat had the Number of the Beast,
and now where Turkey faces the red east,
and the twice-stormed Crimean spit, he cries:
"Rome asked for poets. At her beck and call,
came Lucan, Tacitus and Juvenal,
the *black republicans* who tore the tits
and bowels of the Mother Wolf to bits—
Then psychopath and soldier waved the rod
of empire over Caesar's salvaged bog . . .
Imperial Tiber, Oh my yellow dog,
black earth by the black Roman sea, I lie
with the boy-crazy daughter of the God,
il Duce Augusto. I shall never die."

Our mountain-climbing train had come to earth.
Tired of the querulous hush-hush of the wheels,
the blear-eyed ego kicking in my berth
lay still, and saw Apollo plant his heels
on terra firma through the morning's thigh—
each backward wasted Alp, a Parthenon,
fire-branded socket of the cyclops' eye . . .
There are no tickets to that altitude,
once held by Hellas when the Goddess stood,
prince, pope, philosopher and golden bough,
pure mind and murder at the scything prow—
Minerva the mis-carriage of the brain . . .

Now Paris, our black classic, breaking up
like killer kings on an Etruscan cup.

July in Washington

The stiff spokes of this wheel
touch the sore spots of the earth.

On the Potomac, swan-white
power launches keep breasting the sulphurous wave.

Otters slide and dive and slick back their hair,
raccoons clean their meat in the creek.

On the circles, green statues ride like South American
liberators above the breeding vegetation—

prongs and spearheads of some equatorial
backland that will inherit the globe.

The elect, the elected . . . they come here bright as dimes,
and die dishevelled and soft.

We cannot name their names, or number their dates—
circle on circle, like rings on a tree—

but we wish the river had another shore,
some further range of delectable mountains,

distant hills powdered blue as a girl's eyelid.
It seems the least little shove would land us there,

that only the slightest repugnance of our bodies
we no longer control could drag us back.

Buenos Aires

In my room at the Hotel Continentál
a thousand miles from nowhere,
I heard
the bulky, beefy breathing of the herds.

Cattle furnished my new clothes:
my coat of limp, chestnut-colored suede,
my sharp shoes
that hurt my toes.

A false fin de siecle decorum
snored over Buenos Aires
lost in the pampas
and run by the barracks.

All day I read about newspaper coups d'état
of the leaden, internecine generals—
lumps of dough on the chessboard—and never saw
their countermarching tanks.

Along the sunlit cypress walks
of the Republican martyrs' graveyard,
hundreds of one-room Roman temples
hugged their neo-classical catafalques.

Literal commemorative busts
preserved the frogged coats
and fussy, furrowed foreheads
of those soldier bureaucrats.

By their brazen doors
a hundred marble goddesses
wept like willows. I found rest
by cupping a soft palm to each hard breast.

I was the worse for wear,
and my breath whitened the winter air
next morning, when Buenos Aires filled
with frowning, starch-collared crowds.

Dropping South: Brazil

Walking and walking in a mothy robe,
one finger pushing through the pocket-hole,
I crossed the reading room and met my soul,
hunched, spinning downward on the colored globe.
The ocean was the old Atlantic still,
always the swell greened in, rushed white, and fell,
now warmer than the air. However, there
red flags forbade our swimming. No one swam.
A lawless gentleness. The Latin blonde,
two strips of ribbon, ripened in the sun,
sleeping alone and pillowed on one arm.
No competition. Only rings of boys
butted a ball to keep it in the air,
while inland, people starved, and struck, and died—
unhappy Americas, ah *tristes tropiques!*
and nightly in the gouges by the tide,
macumba candles courted *Yemanjá,*
tall, white, the fish-tailed Virgin of the sea,
corpselike with calla lilies, walking
the water in her white night gown. "I am falling.
Santa Maria, pray for me, I want to stop,
but I have lost my foothold on the map,
now falling, falling, bent, intense, my feet
breaking my clap of thunder on the street."

Soft Wood

(For Harriet Winslow)

Sometimes I have supposed seals
must live as long as the Scholar Gypsy.
Even in their barred pond at the zoo they are happy,
and no sunflower turns
more delicately to the sun
without a wincing of the will.

Here too in Maine things bend to the wind forever.
After two years away, one must get used
to the painted soft wood staying bright and clean,
to the air blasting an all-white wall whiter,
as it blows through curtain and screen
touched with salt and evergreen.

The green juniper berry spills crystal-clear gin,
and even the hot water in the bathtub
is more than water,
and rich with the scouring effervescence
of something healing,
the illimitable salt.

Things last, but sometimes for days here
only children seem fit to handle children,
and there is no utility or inspiration
in the wind smashing without direction.
The fresh paint
on the captains' houses hides softer wood.

Their square-riggers used to whiten
the four corners of the globe,
but it's no consolation to know
the possessors seldom outlast the possessions,
once warped and mothered by their touch.
Shed skin will never fit another wearer.

Yet the seal pack will bark past my window
summer after summer.
This is the season
when our friends may and will die daily.
Surely the lives of the old
are briefer than the young.

Harriet Winslow, who owned this house,
was more to me than my mother.
I think of you far off in Washington,
breathing in the heat wave
and air-conditioning, knowing
each drug that numbs alerts another nerve to pain.

New York 1962: Fragment

(For E.H.L.)

This might be nature—twenty stories high,
two water tanks, tanned shingle, corsetted
by stapled pasture wire, while bed to bed,
we two, one cell here, lie
gazing into the ether's crystal ball,
sky and a sky, and sky, and sky, till death—
my heart stops . . .
This might be heaven. Years ago,
we aimed for less and settled for
a picture, out of style then and now in,
of seven daffodils. We watched them blow:
buttercup yellow were the flowers, and green
the stems as fresh paint, over them the wind,
the blousy wooden branches of the elms,
high summer in the breath that overwhelms
the termites digging in the underpinning . . .
Still over us, still in parenthesis,
this sack of hornets sopping up the flame,
still over us our breath,
sawing and pumping to the terminal,
and down below, we two, two in one waterdrop
vitalised by a needle drop of blood,
up, up, up, up and up,
soon shot, soon slugged into the overflow
that sets the wooden workhorse working here below.

The Flaw

A seal swims like a poodle through the sheet
of blinding salt. A country graveyard, here
and there a rock, and here and there a pine,
throbs on the essence of the gasoline.
Some mote, some eye-flaw, wobbles in the heat,
hair-thin, hair-dark, the fragment of a hair—

a noose, a question? All is possible;
if there's free will, it's something like this hair,
inside my eye, outside my eye, yet free,
airless as grace, if the good God . . . I see.
Our bodies quiver. In this rustling air,
all's possible, all's unpredictable.

Old wives and husbands! Look, their gravestones wait
in couples with the names and half the date—
one future and one freedom. In a flash,
I see us whiten into skeletons,
our eager, sharpened cries, a pair of stones,
cutting like shark-fins through the boundless wash.

Two walking cobwebs, almost bodiless,
crossed paths here once, kept house, and lay in beds.
Your fingertips once touched my fingertips
and set us tingling through a thousand threads.
Poor pulsing *Fête Champêtre!* The summer slips
between our fingers into nothingness.

We too lean forward, as the heat waves roll
over our bodies, grown insensible,
ready to dwindle off into the soul,
two motes or eye-flaws, the invisible . . .
Hope of the hopeless launched and cast adrift
on the great flaw that gives the final gift.

Dear Figure curving like a questionmark,
how will you hear my answer in the dark?

Night Sweat

Work-table, litter, books and standing lamp,
plain things, my stalled equipment, the old broom—
but I am living in a tidied room,
for ten nights now I've felt the creeping damp
float over my pajamas' wilted white . . .
Sweet salt embalms me and my head is wet,
everything streams and tells me this is right;
my life's fever is soaking in night sweat—
one life, one writing! But the downward glide
and bias of existing wrings us dry—
always inside me is the child who died,
always inside me is his will to die—
one universe, one body . . . in this urn
the animal night sweats of the spirit burn.

Behind me! You! Again I feel the light
lighten my leaded eyelids, while the gray
skulled horses whinny for the soot of night.
I dabble in the dapple of the day,
a heap of wet clothes, seamy, shivering,
I see my flesh and bedding washed with light,
my child exploding into dynamite,
my wife . . . your lightness alters everything,
and tears the black web from the spider's sack,
as your heart hops and flutters like a hare.
Poor turtle, tortoise, if I cannot clear
the surface of these troubled waters here,
absolve me, help me, Deart Heart, as you bear
this world's dead weight and cycle on your back.

For the Union Dead

"Relinquunt Omnia Servare Rem Publicam."

The old South Boston Aquarium stands
in a Sahara of snow now. Its broken windows are boarded.
The bronze weathervane cod has lost half its scales.
The airy tanks are dry.

Once my nose crawled like a snail on the glass;
my hand tingled
to burst the bubbles
drifting from the noses of the cowed, compliant fish.

My hand draws back. I often sigh still
for the dark downward and vegetating kingdom
of the fish and reptile. One morning last March,
I pressed against the new barbed and galvanized

fence on the Boston Common. Behind their cage,
yellow dinosaur steamshovels were grunting
as they cropped up tons of mush and grass
to gouge their underworld garage.

Parking spaces luxuriate like civic
sandpiles in the heart of Boston.
A girdle of orange, Puritan-pumpkin colored girders
braces the tingling Statehouse,

shaking over the excavations, as it faces Colonel Shaw
and his bell-cheeked Negro infantry
on St. Gaudens' shaking Civil War relief,
propped by a plank splint against the garage's earthquake.

Two months after marching through Boston,
half the regiment was dead;
at the dedication,
William James could almost hear the bronze Negroes breathe.

Their monument sticks like a fishbone
in the city's throat.
Its Colonel is as lean
as a compass-needle.

He has an angry wrenlike vigilance,
a greyhound's gentle tautness;
he seems to wince at pleasure,
and suffocate for privacy.

He is out of bounds now. He rejoices in man's lovely,
peculiar power to choose life and die—
when he leads his black soldiers to death,
he cannot bend his back.

On a thousand small town New England greens,
the old white churches hold their air
of sparse, sincere rebellion; frayed flags
quilt the graveyards of the Grand Army of the Republic.

The stone statues of the abstract Union Soldier
grow slimmer and younger each year—
wasp-wasted, they doze over muskets
and muse through their sideburns . . .

Shaw's father wanted no monument
except the ditch,
where his son's body was thrown
and lost with his "niggers."

The ditch is nearer.
There are no statues for the last war here;
on Boyleston Street, a commercial photograph
shows Hiroshima boiling

over a Mosler Safe, the "Rock of Ages"
that survived the blast. Space is nearer.
When I crouch to my television set,
the drained faces of Negro school-children rise like balloons.

Colonel Shaw
is riding on his bubble,
he waits
for the blesséd break.

The Aquarium is gone. Everywhere,
giant finned cars nose forward like fish;
a savage servility
slides by on grease.